Athletes Who Made a Difference

COLIN KAEPERNICK

Blake Hoena
illustrated by Sam LeDoyen

Graphic Universe™ • Minneapolis

Graphic Universe™
An imprint of Lerner Publishing Group, Inc.
241 First Avenue North
Minneapolis, MN 55401 USA

For reading levels and more information, look up this title at www.lernerbooks.com.

Main body text set in CCDaveGibbonsLower
Typeface provided by Comicraft

Photo Acknowledgments
The images in this book are used with the permission of: © Michael Zagaris/Getty Images, p. 28 (left);
© ANGELA WEISS/Getty Images, p. 28 (right).

Library of Congress Cataloging-in-Publication Data

Names: Hoena, B. A., author. | Ledoyen, Sam, illustrator. | Graphic Universe (Firm)
Title: Colin Kaepernick : athletes who made a difference / by Blake Hoena ; illustrated by Sam LeDoyen.
Other titles: Making a difference. Athletes who are changing the world.
Description: Minneapolis : Graphic Universe an imprint of Lerner Publishing Group, Inc., 2020. | Series: Athletes
   who made a difference | Includes bibliographical references and index. | Audience: Ages: 8–12 years | Audience:
   Grades: 4–6 | Summary: "This graphic biography traces Colin Kaepernick's road from young sports standout to
   athlete and activist. As Kaepernick protested violence against African Americans, he lost his career in football but
   gained a voice heard worldwide" — Provided by publisher.
Identifiers: LCCN 2019041797 (print) | LCCN 2019041798 (ebook) | ISBN 9781541578173 (Library Binding) |
   ISBN 9781728402932 (Paperback) | ISBN 9781541599420 (eBook)
Subjects: LCSH: Kaepernick, Colin, 1987—-Juvenile literature. | Quarterbacks (Football)—United States—Biography—
   Juvenile literature. | African American football players—United States—Biography—Juvenile literature. | Football
   players—United States—Biography—Juvenile literature. | San Francisco 49ers (Football team)—History—Juvenile
   literature. | Football players—United States—Conduct of life. | Black lives matter movement—Juvenile literature. |
   Political activists—United States—History—Juvenile literature. | Political participation—United States—Juvenile
   literature. | Racism in sports—Juvenile literature. | Sports—Political aspects—Juvenile literature.
Classification: LCC GV939.K25 H65 2020
   (print) | LCC GV939.K25 (ebook) | DDC
   796.332092 [B]—dc23

LC record available at
https://lccn.loc.gov/2019041797
LC ebook record available at
https://lccn.loc.gov/2019041798

Manufactured in the United States of America
3-50108-47798-12/21/2020

Table of Contents

CHAPTER 1
YOUNG KAEPERNICK

During the fall of 1987, 19-year-old Heidi Russo had a difficult decision to make.

I don't know if I can support you—not on my own.

Heidi's boyfriend had left her shortly after she became pregnant.

Heidi gave birth to a son on November 3, 1987, in Milwaukee, Wisconsin.

I'll find you a good home, Colin.

She chose to put him up for adoption. A few weeks later, Heidi met the Kaepernicks.

Heidi, this is Rick and Teresa.

So nice to meet you. Do you have any kids?

Yes, a son, Kyle, and a daughter, Devon.

But doctors said another pregnancy was risky. So, we're hoping to adopt.

Heidi liked the Kaepernicks and believed Colin would have a good life with them. When Colin was five weeks old, Rick and Teresa brought him home to Fond du lac, Wisconsin.

The Kaepernicks stayed in touch with Heidi. They even sent her letters after they moved to Turlock, California, in 1991.

Colin looked different from the rest of the Kaepernicks. He was biracial. His biological father was African American. But Colin still fit right in with his family.

Not everyone understood why he did not look like other members of his family.

Colin knew he was different from the rest of his family.

I'd like you to draw a picture of you and your family.

That's very good, Colin.

This is me.

The Kaepernicks were open with Colin about his adoption. They always made sure he knew he was a part of the family.

It doesn't matter what anyone else thinks, Colin.

You're adopted, but you're still very much our son.

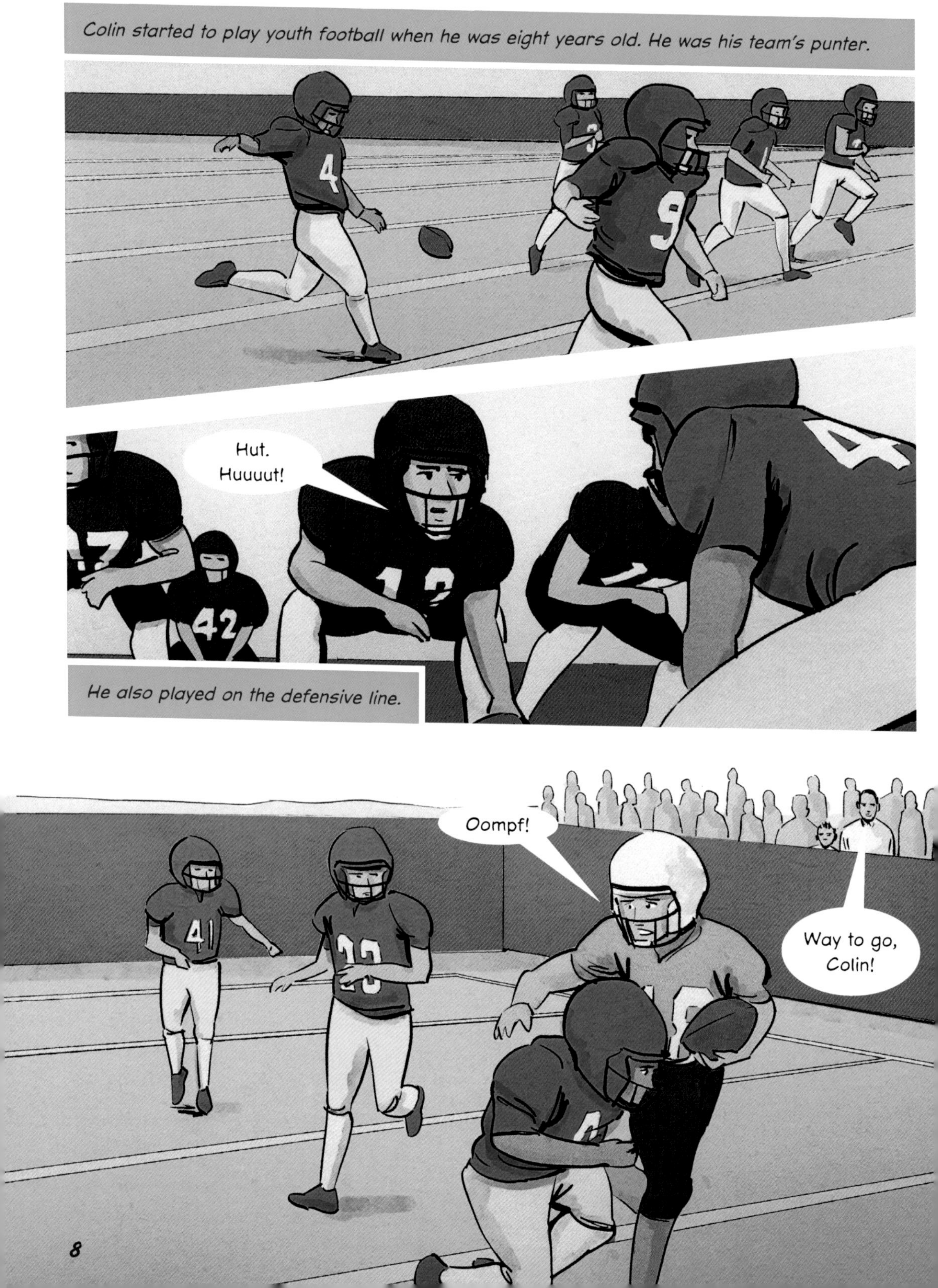
Colin started to play youth football when he was eight years old. He was his team's punter.
Hut. Huuuut!
He also played on the defensive line.
Oompf!
Way to go, Colin!

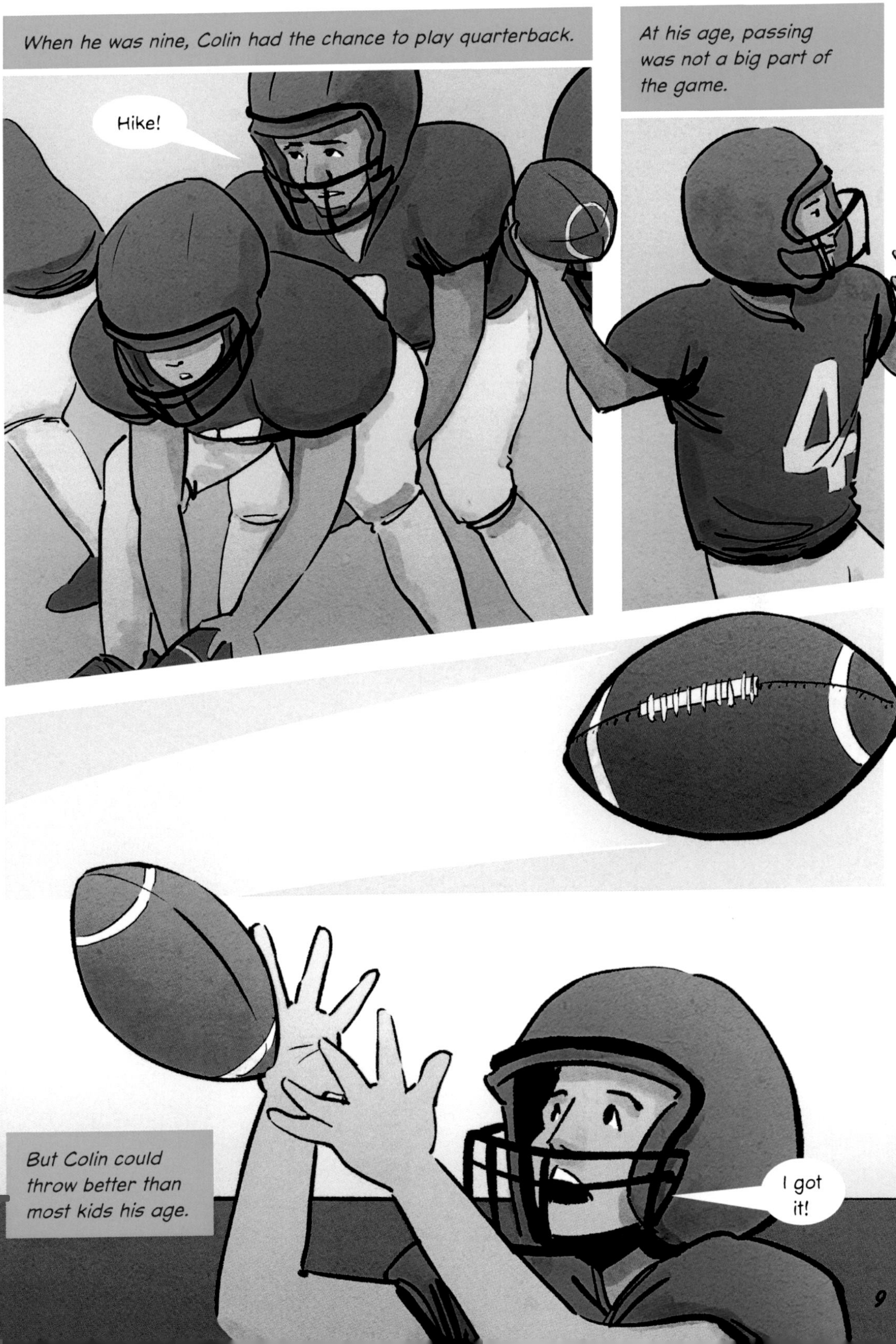

When he was nine, Colin had the chance to play quarterback.
Hike!
At his age, passing was not a big part of the game.
But Colin could throw better than most kids his age.
I got it!

CHAPTER 2

FOOTBALL DREAMS

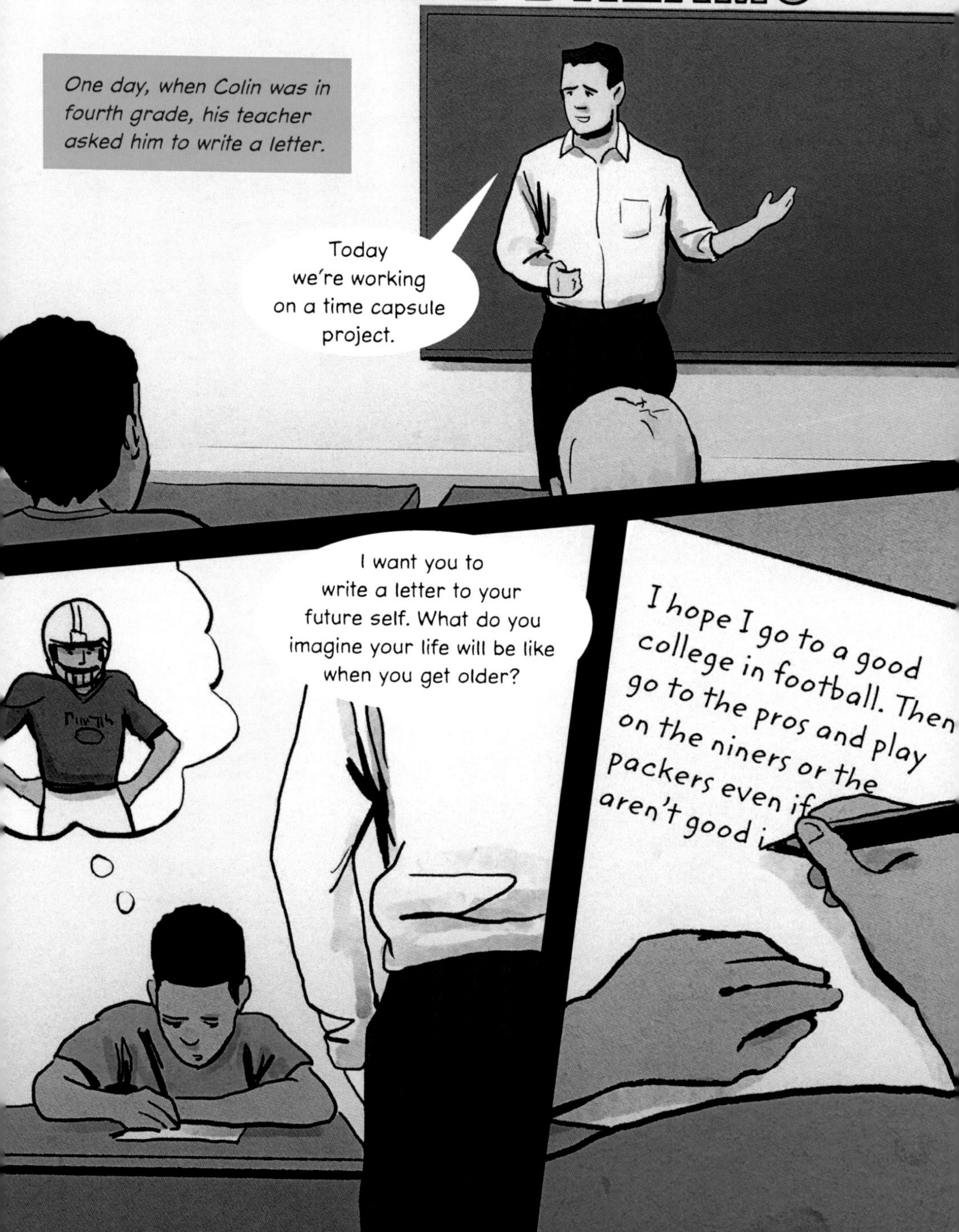

Colin began attending Pitman High School in 2002. He continued to follow his dreams of playing football.

He also played basketball . . .

. . . and baseball.

WHACK!

On top of it all, Colin was a straight-A student.

In his senior year, Colin was the starting quarterback for his high school football team, the Pride.

Kaepernick takes the ball from center . . .

He was tall but very thin. He did not run the ball much because his coach worried he might get hurt being tackled.

. . . he launches it downfield . . .

But he had an incredibly strong arm.

. . . TOUCHDOWN!

In 2005, he led the Pride to the playoffs.

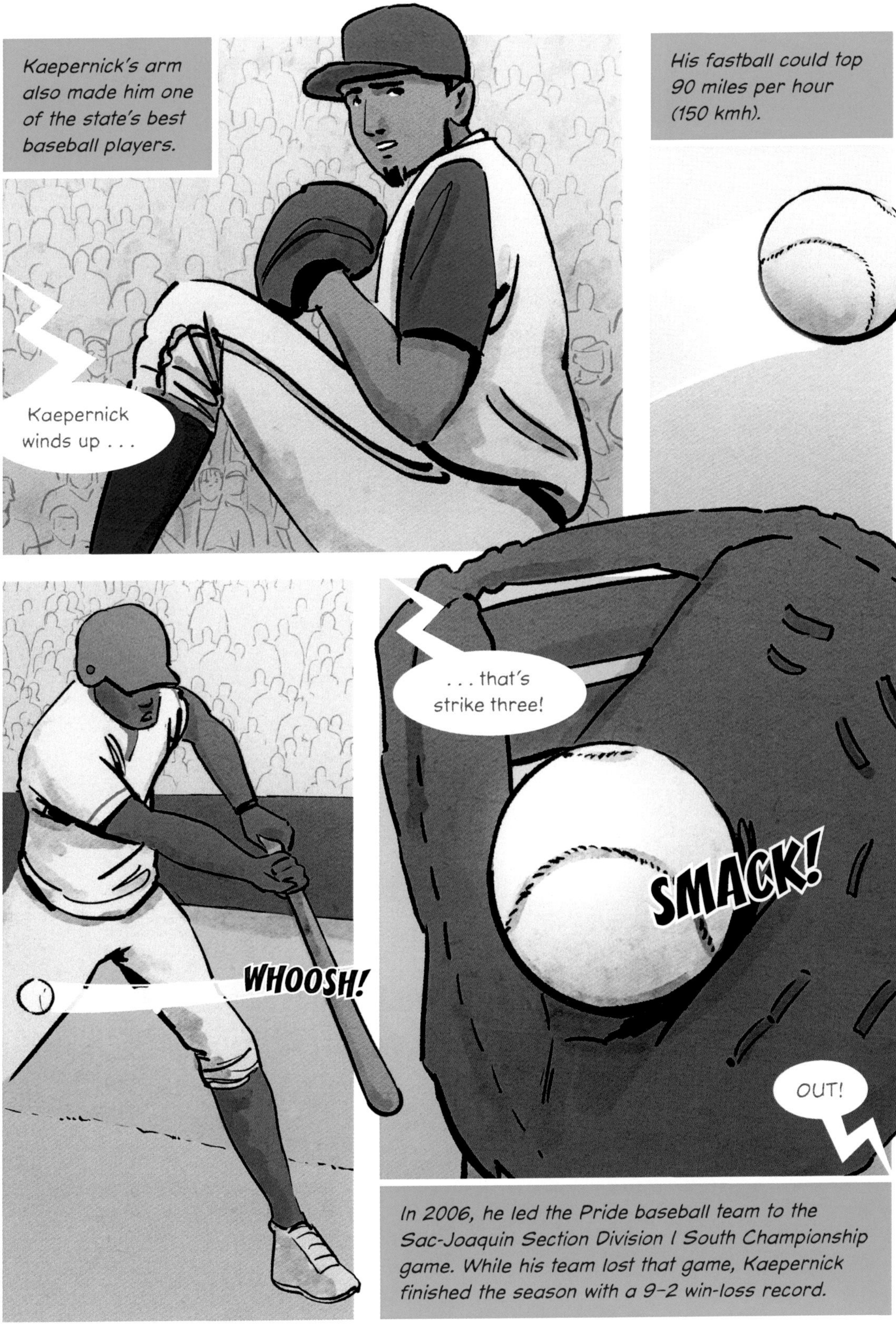

Kaepernick's arm also made him one of the state's best baseball players.
Kaepernick winds up . . .
His fastball could top 90 miles per hour (150 kmh).
WHOOSH!
. . . that's strike three!
SMACK!
OUT!
In 2006, he led the Pride baseball team to the Sac-Joaquin Section Division I South Championship game. While his team lost that game, Kaepernick finished the season with a 9–2 win-loss record.

CHAPTER 3

A RISING STAR

Is that another scholarship offer?

Yeah, from Arizona State.

Colin graduated high school in 2006. His success on the baseball diamond drew a lot of attention from college recruiters.

You want to play football though, don't you?

It's still my dream.

Recruiters were worried Colin was better suited to play baseball. He received little interest from college football teams.

But later in 2006, the University of Nevada–Reno gave Colin a chance to play for the school's football team, the Wolf Pack.

That boy's got a great arm.

Coach Ault was impressed with Colin's arm strength as well as his speed.

We just need to work on your throwing technique.

Colin began as a redshirt freshman. He practiced as a quarterback with the team, but he could not play in games.

Because he was fast, he also learned the position of safety.

On October 6, 2007, the Wolf Pack was playing against Fresno State. Kaepernick was the team's backup quarterback, until . . .

Graziano comes up limping after that sack, and Kaepernick takes the field.

That game, Kaepernick threw four touchdown passes.

Kaepernick tosses his first touchdown for the Wolf Pack!

He rushed for 60 yards and a touchdown.

Kaepernick dives into the end zone from three yards out!

The Wolf Pack lost the game. But from that day on, Kaepernick was the team's starting quarterback.

In 2008, he led the Wolf Pack to a 7–6 record.

Kaepernick to Chris Wellington for six!

In 2009, his team improved to an 8–5 record.

Kaepernick connects with Brandon Wimberly. Touchdown!

Then in 2010, Kaepernick led the Wolf Pack to their best record ever. At 12–1, they earned a spot in the Fight Hunger Bowl.

Kaepernick rushes for the first down!

Kaepernick ended his college career with a 20–13 victory over Boston College.

Kaepernick's success at Nevada readied him for the next step in his football career.

2011

With pick number 36 in the 2011 NFL draft, the San Francisco 49ers select . . .

. . . Colin Kaepernick, quarterback, Nevada.

I can't believe you're going to play for the 49ers!

Once again, he started as a backup quarterback.

Good throw, Alex!

But on November 11, 2012, the 49ers' starting quarterback got hurt. They were losing against the St. Louis Rams when Kaepernick replaced him.

Kaepernick steps back to pass . . .

. . . he takes off running.

Kaepernick rushes for 19 yards and steps out of bounds to stop the clock.

Kaepernick helped his team score two touchdowns. In the final minute of the game, he rushed downfield to set up the tying field goal. The game ended 24-24 in overtime.

CHAPTER 4
AN ATHLETE AND AN ACTIVIST

In 2012, Kaepernick helped lead the 49ers to the playoffs. First, they won against the Green Bay Packers.

Kaepernick steps up. He'll try to run . . . He's got a touchdown!

During the game, Kaepernick rushed for 181 yards, a single-game playoff record for a quarterback.

A week later, the 49ers beat the Atlanta Falcons. The 49ers were headed to the Super Bowl!

But in Super Bowl 47, they lost to the Baltimore Ravens, 34–31.

Kaepernick's got Davis— touchdown!

In 2013, Kaepernick was the 49ers' starting quarterback. The team reached the playoffs but later lost to the Seattle Seahawks.

As the 2014 football season was gearing up, two tragic deaths made national headlines.

These deaths fueled Black Lives Matter protests. Black Lives Matter was founded in 2013. The organization grew from outrage over police violence against African Americans.

While Kaepernick had a great start to his career, the next couple of years were a struggle. In 2014, the 49ers finished with an 8–8 record and missed the playoffs.

Then in 2015 . . .

How's the shoulder feeling?

Still sore, Coach.

Kaepernick's season ended early when he was placed on the IR.

Meanwhile, police officers shot and killed more than thirty unarmed African American men during that year. In response to these deaths, the Black Lives Matter movement continued to grow.

We need justice for all!

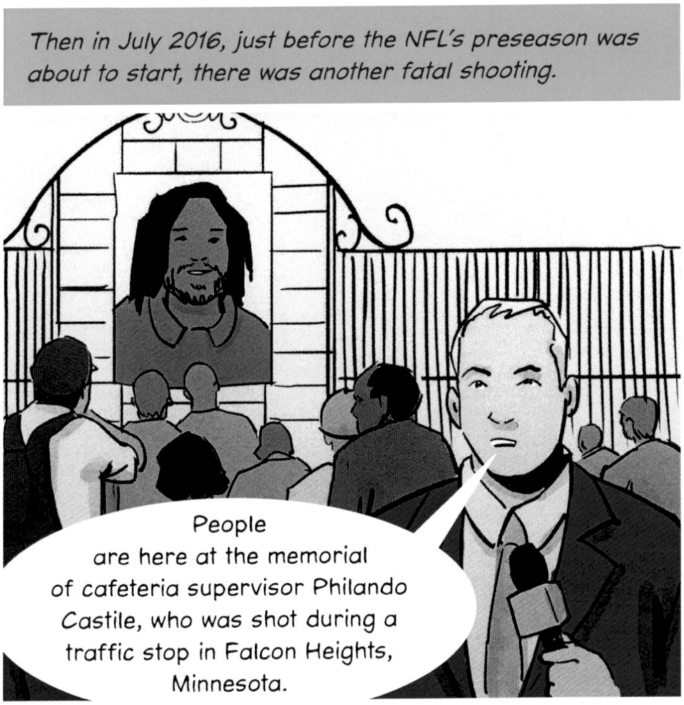

Then in July 2016, just before the NFL's preseason was about to start, there was another fatal shooting.
People are here at the memorial of cafeteria supervisor Philando Castile, who was shot during a traffic stop in Falcon Heights, Minnesota.

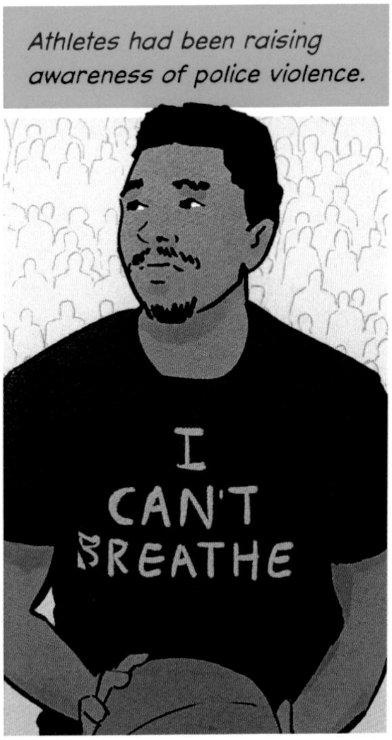

Athletes had been raising awareness of police violence.
I CAN'T BREATHE

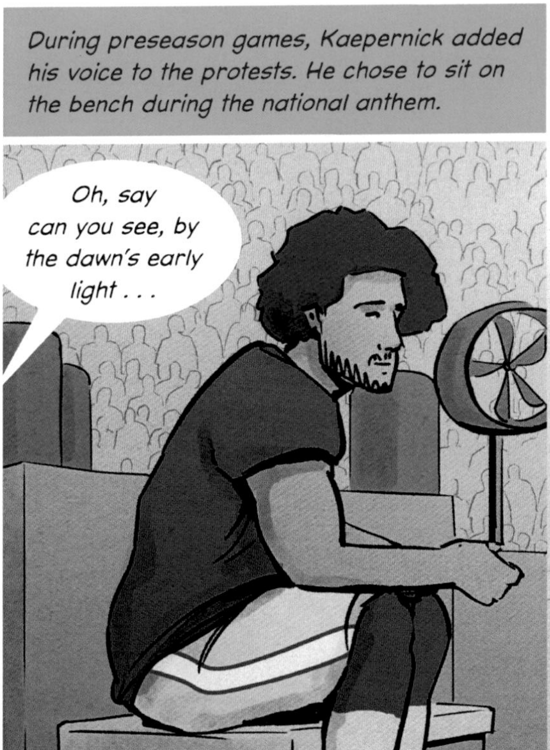

During preseason games, Kaepernick added his voice to the protests. He chose to sit on the bench during the national anthem.
Oh, say can you see, by the dawn's early light . . .

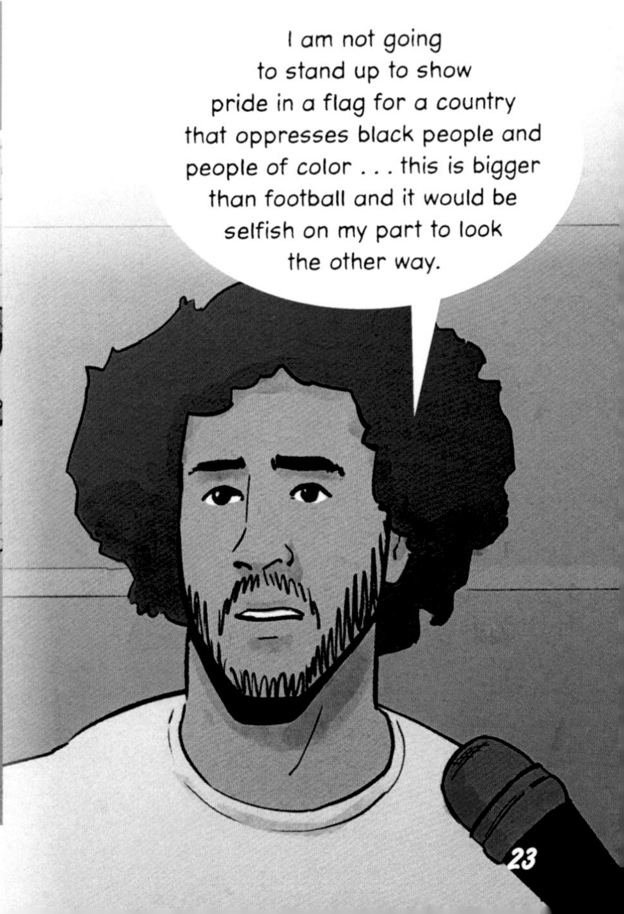

I am not going to stand up to show pride in a flag for a country that oppresses black people and people of color . . . this is bigger than football and it would be selfish on my part to look the other way.

Many people thought Kaepernick was being unpatriotic and disrespectful of people who served in the US military. So, he spoke to Nate Boyer, a former NFL player and US army veteran.

I want to make sure I'm not hurting those who fought for our country.

If you aren't going to stand, why not take a knee instead? It's how we show respect to fallen soldiers.

On September 1, during the 49ers first exhibition game of the 2016 season, Kaepernick knelt during the national anthem. His teammate, Eric Reid, joined him.

. . . What so proudly we hail'd at the twilight's last gleaming? . . .

Soon, players on other NFL teams were joining in Kaepernick's protest.

. . . Whose broad stripes and bright stars through the perilous fight . . .

The 49ers ended 2016 with a 2–14 record. It was Kaepernick's worst season with the team. Kaepernick left the 49ers after the season's end.

But the kneeling protests Kaepernick started continued without him. They spread to college and high school teams . . .

. . . and even to other sports.

. . . O'er the ramparts we watch'd were so gallantly streaming? . . .

. . . And the rocket's red glare, the bombs bursting in air . . .

Meanwhile, the protests inspired the Take A Knee hashtag.

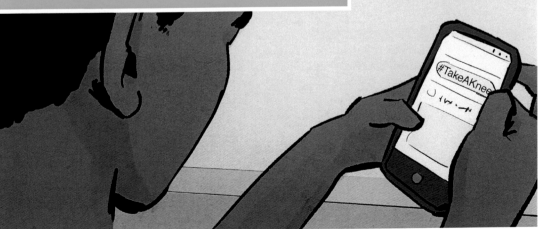

#TakeAKnee

The protests that Kaepernick inspired were controversial. Almost everyone had an opinion on the Take A Knee movement.

Anyone who kneels is disrespecting the people who serve this country!

It's their first amendment right to speak out against injustices.

Football players should stick to football, not politics.

The US military fights to defend our rights, including the right to protest!

As arguments over Take A Knee raged on, Kaepernick was left without work in the NFL. After he became a free agent, no other NFL team chose to sign him. Kaepernick's supporters argued that his activism was the reason why.

There's a lot of people out there that don't want to see you succeed.

But he had other ways to reach people. In 2016, Kaepernick had founded the Know Your Rights Camp. Through this movement, he continues to guide and empower young people to fight, as he did, for positive change.

But the people in this room do.

He sacrificed his football career by speaking out against racial oppression. But in the struggle, Kaepernick found a new mission.

AFTERWORD

Colin Kaepernick has not played in the NFL since the 2016 season. In 2017, he filed a lawsuit against the NFL. He claimed that because of his protests, NFL teams colluded to prevent him from playing again. The lawsuit was settled in early 2019 for an undisclosed sum of money.

Since Kaepernick first took a knee, his activism has made a huge impact. He helped draw the nation's attention to racial issues that had long been ignored. He used his platform as an athlete to speak out and inspire others to do the same. In doing so, Kaepernick took a personal and professional risk. In response to his courage, he was named an Ambassador of Conscience by human rights organization Amnesty International in 2018.

Through his Know Your Rights Camp, Kaepernick has set his sights on helping young people. His organization teaches them how to interact safely and properly with law enforcement. It also helps promote healthy living and education. Kaepernick hopes to empower future generations to know and stand up for their rights.

ATHLETE SNAPSHOT

BIRTH NAME: Colin Rand Kaepernick

NICKNAME: Kap

BORN: November 3, 1987, Milwaukee, Wisconsin

Awards of Note

◆ 2008 and 2010—Western Athletic Conference Offensive Player of the Year

◆ 2013—Most Rushing Yards by a Quarterback in a playoff game: 181

◆ 2013—ESPY Award for Best Breakthrough Athlete

◆ 2017—Sports Illustrated Muhammad Ali Legacy Award

◆ 2018—Amnesty International Ambassador of Conscience Award

SOURCE NOTES

10   Turlock Journal—Colin Kaepernick
https://www.turlockjournal.com/sports/college/colin-kaepernick-past-present-and-future/

23   SBNation
https://www.sbnation.com/2016/8/27/12669890/colin-kaepernick-49ers-nfl-national-anthem-seated

27   Facebook—Colin Kaepernick
https://www.facebook.com/kaepernick7/videos/1224322424288664/?v=1224322424288664

GLOSSARY

biracial: having parents of different ethnicities

draft: the process of selecting players for a team

field goal: in football, a kick between an opposing team's goal posts. A field goal scores three points.

first down: the first in a set of four downs that a football team gets to move the ball ten yards down field

intercepted: when a quarterback's pass is caught by an opposing player

IR: Injured Reserve; teams put players on IR to free up their roster spot while also keeping the player on the team

punter: a type of kicker in football

recruiter: a person seeking to find the best players for a sports team

scholarship: money a college offers to players to join their sports teams

strangulation: the act of being choked

time capsule: a container holding items from the past

FURTHER INFORMATION

Black Lives Matter
https://blacklivesmatter.com

Braun, Eric. *The Civil Rights Movement*. Minneapolis: Lerner Publications, 2019.

Colin Kaepernick
https://kaepernick7.com

Colin Kaepernick NFL stats
https://www.pro-football-reference.com/players/K/KaepCo00.htm

Fishman, Jon M. *Colin Kaepernick*. Minneapolis: Lerner Publications, 2015.

Know Your Rights Camp
https://knowyourrightscamp.com

Military.com—U.S. Flag Code
https://www.military.com/flag-day/us-flag-code.html

San Francisco 49ers
https://www.49ers.com

INDEX